EVENINGS WITH IDRIES SHAH

Books by Idries Shah

Sufi Studies and Middle Eastern Literature
The Sufis
Caravan of Dreams
The Way of the Sufi
Tales of the Dervishes: *Teaching-stories Over a
Thousand Years*
Sufi Thought and Action

**Traditional Psychology,
Teaching Encounters and Narratives**
Thinkers of the East: *Studies in Experientialism*
Wisdom of the Idiots
The Dermis Probe
Learning How to Learn: *Psychology and Spirituality
in the Sufi Way*
Knowing How to Know
The Magic Monastery: *Analogical and Action Philosophy*
Seeker After Truth
Observations
Evenings with Idries Shah
The Commanding Self

University Lectures
A Perfumed Scorpion (Institute for the Study of
Human Knowledge and California University)
Special Problems in the Study of Sufi Ideas
(Sussex University)
The Elephant in the Dark: *Christianity,
Islam and the Sufis* (Geneva University)
Neglected Aspects of Sufi Study: *Beginning to Begin*
(The New School for Social Research)
Letters and Lectures of Idries Shah

Current and Traditional Ideas
Reflections
The Book of the Book
A Veiled Gazelle: *Seeing How to See*
Special Illumination: *The Sufi Use of Humour*

The Mulla Nasrudin Corpus
The Pleasantries of the Incredible Mulla Nasrudin
The Subtleties of the Inimitable Mulla Nasrudin
The Exploits of the Incomparable Mulla Nasrudin
The World of Nasrudin

Travel and Exploration
Destination Mecca

Studies in Minority Beliefs
The Secret Lore of Magic
Oriental Magic

Selected Folktales and Their Background
World Tales

A Novel
Kara Kush

Sociological Works
Darkest England
The Natives Are Restless
The Englishman's Handbook

Translated by Idries Shah
The Hundred Tales of Wisdom (Aflaki's *Munaqib*)

EVENINGS WITH IDRIES SHAH

Idries Shah

ISF PUBLISHING

ISBN 978-1-78479-210-7

First published 1981
Published in this edition 2019

Requests for permission to reprint, reproduce etc., to:
The Permissions Department
ISF Publishing
The Idries Shah Foundation
P. O. Box 71911
London NW2 9QA
United Kingdom
permissions@isf-publishing.org

In association with The Idries Shah Foundation

The Idries Shah Foundation is a registered charity in
the United Kingdom
Charity No. 1150876

Evenings with Idries Shah

THESE MATERIALS, AS those will know who have read compilations of discussion sessions with Rumi and other Sufis, form a part of a valuable and for most people an unusual body of literature.

Traditionally, Sufi exponents give out ideas and stories, give answers to some questions, prescribe exercises and at times their letters and lectures are also circulated.

During evening meetings, for many centuries, the performance which involves both talking to the audience and interacting with its members has what is experienced as a unique quality.

If recorded Sufi materials cannot substitute for actual presence at a Sufi school, they can certainly prepare for it. Indeed, so many barriers to understanding are removed that afterwards one can learn both faster and more surely in subsequent efforts.

So this is not merely 'a kiss sent by messenger': it is the extract of a number of highly profitable meetings.

R. Easterling
K. Hanafy

Nature and Discipline

TWO SUFIS WERE agreeing that almost the whole of life was a struggle between nature and discipline, and how there had to be a third course, directed study, which avoided either while allowing both to operate.

A certain student, anxious to learn but schooled in the false theories of mere tonguesters, said:

'First, why can discipline alone, or nature alone, not lead to knowledge? Second, how can you show that so much of human life and time is wasted in the interplay of the two?'

The Sufis only answered:

'We shall demonstrate this to you when the time is ripe.'

After a time, the Sufis asked the student to accompany them on a journey.

Before they set off, the First Sufi said, privately, to the young man:

'I shall take a bag of dried dates, to allow for the needs of nature, which demands that the body be nourished with food.'

The Second Sufi, also privately, said to him:

'I shall show you how nature is defied by training!'

They travelled far, and whenever the First Sufi became hungry, the Second Sufi asked him a question.

The first time it was:

'Who is that man over there?'

Now the First Sufi, from politeness, had to put the date out of his mouth so that he could answer; even though, in this case, it was only to say: 'I do not remember who he is.' This happened three times. The second time, when asked: 'What is the name of that village?', the First Sufi said: 'I do not know.' The third time, when asked: 'How far have we still to go?', he answered, 'I have not calculated it.'

Eventually they arrived at a spot where a beautiful girl was sitting by a well, where she had been drawing water. The Second Sufi said:

'I shall go and talk to her. You stay here and whistle if her people appear to take her back to her village, for they do not like strangers talking to their womenfolk hereabouts.'

So the student and the First Sufi stayed on guard. They watched while their companion spoke to the girl and then, just as she was beginning to smile at him, the First Sufi whistled.

The Second Sufi came running back, asking:

'What is it?'

The First Sufi said:

'I have just remembered the name of that man you asked me about on the road. His name was Halim.'

'How dare you trouble me at a time like this?' cried the Second Sufi, and he went back to the girl.

Presently, when the man and the girl were deep in conversation, the First Sufi whistled again, and again the other man came running. 'What is it?' he asked.

'That village you wondered about. It was called Nimgil...'

'Why don't you leave me alone!' asked the other indignantly. And he went back to the girl.

The watchers could just see in the twilight that the young woman was laughing at something which the Second Sufi had said, when the First Sufi whistled a third time. At first he did not want to leave the girl, but the Second Sufi could not take the risk of being caught by her kinsfolk, so he came back running. As soon as he reached them, the First Sufi said: 'I have just worked out that we are three-quarters the way along on our journey...'

At that moment the three men saw that the villagers had arrived at the well, and were taking the girl away with them.

Then the two Sufis turned to the student and said in unison:

'Now do you see the problems and the time taken, and the uselessness, of the struggle between nature and discipline?'

Overdose

Q: Why, and how, is it that Sufi writings seem to show intense spirituality at times, and then, at other times, what looks like the reverse? Sufi teachers will seemingly preach deep religious concepts at one moment, and then be found removing emotional attitudes?

A: I should have thought that that was quite obvious. Apparently it is not, so I will tell you. Here is an analogy:

If a lifeguard jumps into the water and fishes out a man who is drowning, does this imply any criticism of the art of swimming? If the lifeguard reverses the swimming process (by bringing the man back to land and keeping him out of the water and the water out of him) does this mean that the lifeguard does not teach swimming or advocate being in the water?

Your problem is that the Sufis can see when there is an overdose of something; and they know what to do about it. But a doctor treating an overdose should not be mistaken for a man who disapproves of medicine. At one moment he administers a medicine, at another he works against the motive of medicine.

What I regard as most illuminating about this question is that it has to be asked at all; because, by asking it, the questioner has shown how deficient and unobjective is the background of information and conceptions which are his only endowment.

Monarch and Artist

IT IS RELATED among the wise that there was once an emperor who desired a piece of calligraphy to hang upon a wall. He asked seven of his advisers as to who could execute it; and they recommended a certain superb penman, who produced very little, though all his work was supremely excellent.

'See what he can do,' said the ruler, and so the seven visited the famous man in his studio. He accepted the commission, promising that the work would be ready as soon as possible.

After several months without hearing from the artist, the courtiers went to his house, to see how he was progressing.

'I have not started yet,' said the man, 'because I have to go through a period of meditation, to prepare myself to fulfil a Royal command.'

When the delegation, afraid that the monarch might call for the picture at any time, called upon their man again, this time three months later, he merely said: 'I have not yet started: I am purging my mind of unnecessary thought, through reveries.'

Month after month passed. Concentration (to focus his mind), contemplation (to attune to the Infinite), and many other states and stages were entered into and passed by the devout and talented calligrapher, but there was still no product of his genius.

Finally the grandees, hovering between awe of this man's amazing and impressive discipline and a growing conviction that they could be punished at any moment if their master suddenly remembered their task and asked for the work, arrived at the artist's door to have the matter out with him for the last time.

No less than three years had passed; they found him ready; and they saw that he was seated at a drawing-board, with a clean piece of paper before him. As they watched, he raised his pen and applied it to the surface.

In less time than it takes to tell, the most beautiful design which any of them had seen was seen to be inscribed.

Ecstatically gathering up this treasure, the visitors showered gold upon the artist and hastened to the palace.

They went directly to the hall of audience, where they found the Emperor sitting, resplendently attired as if for a special occasion, sitting on his throne and surrounded by the aristocrats, the military commanders, the ministers and ambassadors, governors of provinces and other high officials of the realm. The seven emissaries took up their ceremonial positions in due order of seniority and distinction.

The Emperor, as if reading their thoughts, said:

'Gentlemen! I hope that you have been able to bring us the work of the Master Calligrapher, a desire for whose possession was expressed to you some years ago.'

Astonished at the coincidence, and at the same time delighted to be able to discharge their trust, the seven advisers stepped forward as one, their leader unrolling the breathtaking masterwork for all to see.

When the gasps of wonderment at the beauty of the object had somewhat subsided, the ruler thanked his faithful retainers and asked them to withdraw, with the picture, to an adjoining chamber, where they were to receive their rewards.

A hidden orchestra played sweet music and rare foods and drinks were brought as the advisers were ushered to their luxurious divans by no less an individual than the Lord High Chamberlain, who handed them sacks of precious jewels and accorded them every honour.

Suddenly, however, the seven men noticed, suspended on the wall of this room and revealed by a curtain which was slowly parting, a piece of calligraphy which appeared identical to the one which they had obtained with so much effort and anxiety, and which had involved such time and so much dedication on the part of the artist.

Their mouths opening and shutting like fish under water, they severally gasped, 'Who, how ,why, what, when?'

'If you are enquiring about that perfect work of art, O splendid and utterly wise counsellors,' said the Chamberlain, 'know that it was dashed off in a matter of seconds by our lord his Imperial Majesty, some three years ago, while illustrating approximately the kind of work which he hoped might be obtained from a competent artist, to embellish one of his rooms.'

'But it took us three years of suffering to have this one made,' spluttered the leader of the advisers; 'furthermore, it required the artist to discipline himself with the utmost rigour, with fasting and purges, vegetarianism and mantrams, recitations and readings, concentration and contemplation...'

'I rather fancy,' said their host, 'that the artist was disciplining himself at your expense and at the expense of his Majesty. Now the Monarch, on the other hand, had already so prepared himself and had gone through the necessary deprivations, so that nobody was exploited when he desired to exercise his own art. The artist may be a great one, but he is still learning. Our Ruler already has learnt.'

Unknown Capacities
of Man

Q: The Western psychologists (and here I have in mind Sigmund Freud especially) have given us interesting and operable tools for observation. Many of their theories are in question, but the tools remain. If I see someone constantly avoiding something, for instance, I can infer from it that he has had some early experience which caused this aversion. I can understand another person when he is using 'rationalisation', because Freud has given me the explanation and the procedure to approach this question. The advantage is that it not only explains the other person's behaviour to me but also enables me to become less annoyed or inefficient in my dealing with him. Can we find similar advantages in Eastern, especially Sufi, observation and learning, which can be applied to day-to-day activities?

A: It would be extremely peculiar, I think, if you could *not* find such things. Whether you are prepared to use them is the question which interests me most.

Q: May I have an example of one such technique?

A: One of the most useful is the fact that you may 'pick up' from another person, without his being aware that you are doing so, or that he can do it, information which is being received by his mind. To clarify: there may be a subject of mutual interest in which someone is asking you questions, and you may get the answer because you can register his awareness of the answer, while he cannot himself do so.

Q: Is this something like 'mediumship'?

A: Only very slightly like it, because in the cases of 'mediumship' generally investigated in the West, there is a great deal of belief that messages are coming from the dead, and also too much inefficiency; for example, the 'messages' are more often than not completely banal and serve only social purposes.

Q: Do you mean that there is a great deal of information 'in the air' and that this can be obtained through meetings of people, and that people are almost always unaware of this?

A: Yes.

Q: *What prevents people making use of this technique?*

A: The same thing that prevents people from understanding and using 'mediumistic' procedures. In the first place, they are emotionally attracted and are taking social satisfactions from the situation, which prevents it working accurately, in the second, they cannot detach their 'greed' and self-centredness from it, so they only want things which they desire. They do not want information or experience for its own sake. So the element behind this phenomenon simply yields whatever it can under these most limiting circumstances.

Q: So people should approach this matter more sincerely and genuinely?

A: Exactly.

Q: And this form of communication does not operate without that sincerity?

A: This form of communication is operating all the time. People are not aware of it. If it were not working, man would not have the information and relative efficiency which he has. In the absence of sincerity the lack of greed will allow much to happen which will help the individual, even though he will not be able to say how this happened, and will therefore put all sorts of choices and happenings down to chance, luck and judgement.

The Importance of Grouping

THE RIGHT PEOPLE at the right place at the right time (*Zaman – Makan – Ikhwan*) has many reasons. One of the most important of these is that if you group people wrongly, you exaggerate their undesirable characteristics. Although not so rapid nor so publicly visible, you can get a similar effect to the proneness of a mass of people to become a mob. Just as a random collection of people assembled around an oversimplified issue easily becomes a mindless mob, irrational and even destructive, so may people collected together, without adequate preparation and safeguards, become a corroding factor in spiritual matters. They may damage themselves or others. Familiar examples are the abnormal enmities and exaggerated behaviour of members of coteries, whether these be scholars or professionals, in many societies, both current and ancient, as well as the numerous religious groupings which go sour.

Although this behaviour abounds – narrow-mindedness, poor understanding, lack of generosity to others outside the 'in-group' – few people, it seems, realise that it is so widespread. Fewer still have bothered to see it as a matter of study. And yet fewer seem to imagine, when you mention it to them, that it is avoidable by planning. At the best, in my experience, such people merely assume that it cannot happen to them.

And yet, by not looking at it, how many opportunities of learning about this thing are missed! If people won't *look*, merely telling them that something is there will not suffice. The purpose of talking about it, then, is not to add to the stock of formal information on the subject: it is rather to stimulate curiosity among whoever hears or reads, so that he may make this a verified part of his own experience. Experience teaches.

Derivative

Q: What is to prevent people from choosing the best ideas from all kinds of teachings, and adopting them?

A: What prevents ignorant people doing this is their incapacity. What prevents insightful ones is lack of necessity. People who know how to do it do not have to attempt it, because when one has this knowledge the activity is superfluous, because one then has access to the material which corresponds best to the time, place and people, without having to synthesise. Synthesisers are the half-ignorant.

The amalgams of various teachings which are believed to provide new syntheses 'for modern man' are mere conglomerations of formulations which, by producing a kind of mixture, have altered the dynamic of all of them.

The analogy might be with the assembling of pieces of formulae or equations or houses or instruments without understanding what part each fragment has had to play. The result may appear interesting, but it is ineffective.

The ancient sages have supplied us with a good reference to this situation, alluding to the pride which adheres to ancestry (of people or ideas) while ignoring other, equally or more significant aspects:

A mule, they relate, was asked who his parents were. He replied, 'Well, my *mother* was a pedigreed champion...'

What Prevents Learning?

THE ORDINARY, FAMILIAR Self, which is a secondary one, is easily conditioned, dominated and operated by primitive logic. People thus make decisions based on habit, on command or upon lack of information. They do this because they are trained to act in this way, and also because they frequently lack flexibility of approach.

Such workings of the human mind, in the three modes just given, can be isolated and examined by taking them separately and clothing them in individual human terms. This is one of the functions of narrative-instruction.

The materials for this study are almost everywhere, but they lack, in most societies, an organiser. Let us take three anecdotes and examine the working of the various disabilities:

First, we may say that people fail to do things towards learning because they are under the domination of a belief or an institution, which inculcates a habit of only thinking in one way. The first story concerns a man who lives in a totalitarian country. He is sitting in the dentist's chair. The dentist says: 'Open your mouth...'

'What?' answers the patient. 'And get shot?'

This caricature shows the literalness of the effect on people of a dominating institution or idea. In societies, for instance, where the tradition is that people cannot know more about themselves because that is a reserved area confined to, say, priests or seers, the subconscious belief is that one must not attempt to go further.

This behaviour is sometimes imagined to be duty or proper behaviour. It is useful enough in the right place, but positively disabling where flexibility is needed.

The official barriers may be institutions, traditions or social norms, producing what contemporary psychologists call an inhibition.

The second peculiarity of the mind which can be incarnated in a story to illustrate primitive logic is where the individual tries to do something without knowing the way to do it: indeed, he may imagine that the means which he adopts is the only possible way.

Mulla Nasrudin, it is related, was drowned, and an angel came to put him through the customary examination.

'How did it happen?' he asked.

'I was crossing from France to England,' said the Mulla.

'And the boat sank?'

The Mulla was amazed. 'You mean there is a *boat*?' he said.

This primitive sense, that one wants something and therefore must be able to get it or do it, lurks in everyone, and is an integral component of the Secondary Self.

Again it is useful in the right place, for it enables effort to be made: but it is disastrous when it operates randomly, as the Mulla found out.

The third characteristic is that of habit: excellent in its own place, but cripplingly limiting where it will not work.

The tale which covers this aspect of the mind's working is no less amusing for being a modern hybrid. It concerns a dedicated organiser of industrial action, shown into the presence of a spiritual master.

He put his hands over his ears.

When he was leaving, a disciple said:

'You won't get very far that way...'

'I don't care,' said the visitor, 'I'm on strike.'

Conditioning, habit, proves counter-productive where it operates automatically and again, lacks flexibility.

So, in this way, we can observe the composite influence which effectively cuts people off from knowledge: a Self which, when used for certain purposes, is excellent; but whose operation may be useless and even harmful when applied to areas which are irrelevant to it.

Thus the three elements: duty, ignorance and habit, in the absence of a 'switching mechanism' turn the individual into a prisoner. No wonder he constantly asks how he can escape. It is a little less obvious why, in trying to escape, he turns to one or other of the methods which entrap him as means to freedom.

Eastern Cults

*Q: Legitimate Sufi study is anything
but a cult; but what is to be the eventual
effect of the imported Eastern ones on
the West?*

A: People import the most peculiar
cults from the East, clean them up a
little, and package them for use in the
West. When people from Europe and
America go eastwards, they usually
become rather silent about what
they have found, on their return. If
they only knew how one animal can
appear to be another, as in a famous
joke, they might think twice before
getting involved. Because there are few
admonitions about this matter already

in Western culture – on the whole only threats from bigots trying to preserve their own frightful cults – people don't suspect the dangers until the cult has done its work.

We have found it useful to use a gentler, allegorical method. I quote the dog-fight legend:

There was once a man walking a very funny-looking dog who met another man with a champion bulldog, in some fields.

'I bet you my dog can beat yours,' said the owner of the bulldog.

'Not likely,' challenged the other man. So they started them fighting, for a wager.

Within three minutes the strange beast had practically eaten the bulldog alive.

Paying his money over, the bulldog's master said: 'That's a very strange-looking animal you have there – mustard-coloured, with a huge face...'

'Yes,' said the other man, 'but you should have seen him before I cut off his mane and clipped his tail...'

We shall see, in the West, what the result is to be when the 'lion' starts to maraud...

Spiritual Exercises

Q: How is it that so many people seem to become unhinged when they carry out spiritual exercises laid down by gurus and other teachers? If people are overdoing things, what of the proverb: 'If a lot of something is bad, a little of it is also bad'?

A: It is all a matter of measure, as in everything. If you took even the multiplication tables and used them when you did not need them, you might become abnormal.

Have you not heard the Kashmiri story of the farmer who got all his grain in and found that he had only enough for ten months' food?

He said to himself:

'This means that I lack food for two months of this ensuing year. It is best to get the worst over first.'

So he decided to fast for two months, after which he would have food for ten months.

Naturally, fasting for so long, he died. So he lost his life, and did not need the remainder of the grain.

The Sentry and the Vault

A POWERFUL KING was entering his palace amid a concourse of soldiers, his personal guard, whose accoutrements gleamed with silver, gold and precious gems.

As he was passing, a sentry, who believed that such manifestations of wealth and power were vain and foolish, was overcome by these reflections and shouted: 'If you have wealth, you can do anything! Wealth is all you need! There is nothing but appearance and show, and those things are bought with treasure!'

The soldier was seized and taken to where the King sat on his throne.

'Are you convinced that all that anyone needs is to be surrounded by wealth, and that wealth is power?' asked the King.

'Yes, I am!' said the sentry, who had given up all hope for his life.

'In that case,' said the King, 'I am prepared to try an experiment. You shall have all the wealth you can imagine.'

He ordered that the soldier be placed in a vault and that he be surrounded with bricks of gold and silver, and have sacks of jewels piled around him. Then the vault was to be bricked up.

Now it so happened that a certain dervish was present at Court on that day, and he heard the verdict and the orders being given for the soldier's immurement. When the man had been sealed in his prison, the dervish approached it by night and carefully, quietly made a small hole in the wall of the vault, so that he could speak to the soldier. He whispered: 'I have started the process. Now it is for you to see what will happen, and how your destiny may go from here.'

The soldier was surprised, but he was somewhat grateful for having some sort of communication with the real world outside. After a day or two, when he was getting very hungry, he began to shout down the hole in the wall, and his voice happened to come to the ears of a goldsmith who was passing.

The goldsmith went to the hole and heard the soldier's story. He went home, brought back a forked stick, and withdrew some of the jewels which the soldier offered him. In this way he supplied the prisoner with food and water day after day, getting paid in jewels.

After some weeks the soldier found that time was hanging very heavily on his hands, and he asked the goldsmith for some metal-working tools. With these he made a flute for himself out of the gold in the vault, and practised melodies which he played, to provide some recreation.

As he played, however, the prisoner began to think, 'I have gold and silver, and jewels, I have food and water and amusement, but I have no freedom.' His tunes became more and more plaintive, and he became more and more wrapped up in them, as his thoughts sought to understand his condition and to probe as to whether he could ever escape.

One day the dervish came past the hole in the wall of the vault to see what was happening.

The soldier said: 'I have everything except freedom. Can you not help me to escape? After all, I have a king's ransom in treasure here, for anyone who will let me out.'

The dervish answered: 'Such are the conditions of this world that I cannot directly help you to escape. If the King were to find out, then I would lose my position at Court, and would not be able to help people as I have, to some extent, helped you. If you want to escape intensely enough, however, you will achieve it.'

And he went away.

The soldier concentrated his mind upon his desire to escape and on his former superficiality in believing that wealth was enough to attain anything, and this had an effect on his music. So powerful and haunting did the flute-playing become that the King, walking nearby one day, was enchanted by it.

He asked what it could be. A search was made, and in the vault, instead of a withered skeleton, the soldier was found alive and well, playing on his golden flute.

When the man was brought before him, the King said:

'And who might you be?'

The soldier said:

'Your Majesty! You will remember that I am the man whom you immured in the vault, with gold and silver, for saying that wealth was everything!'

The King asked: 'And what do you think about things now?'

'I have learnt,' said the soldier, 'that first of all a man needs a friend, like the dervish who made the beginning of my new life possible, and saved me from death. Second, money can be used, as it was useful to the goldsmith, but it is useless without friends. Thirdly, these things are useless without skills, skills are useless without their application, application without recreation, recreation without freedom. But everything, if my experiences are any guide, is useless without the intervention of someone who knows what can be done, and who does it – who "digs the hole in the wall of the vault".'

And so the King released the soldier, and he went on to other adventures, but those are part of another story...

Observation

MANY PEOPLE, HEARING that Sufis are often highly observant, imagine that by developing this faculty, instead of the analogous one of a higher-level observation capacity, they will become wise; and fail to understand that observation is important in relation to the things observed, not to the faculty alone.

In order to correct these impressions, the following story has been told:

A Sufi was a witness in a court case.

The judge said:

'How many steps did this man fall down?'

The Sufi said, 'I don't know.'

'You mean to say that you put yourself forward as a witness,' shouted the judge, 'and you cannot answer a simple question?'

The Sufi said:

'And how long has Your Honour been a judge in this court?'

'Twenty years.'

'And can you tell me the number of beams in the roof of this hall?'

People still behave absurdly, in spite of such instructional tales. As a wise man once said: 'If anyone delights in mud, clear water will not attract him.'

Running A Study Group

Q: What is the best qualification for running a study group?

A: Common sense. If one has this, and works carefully with the materials, a sensitivity is developed which becomes the permanent qualification or capacity.

You would be surprised how many people show that they are not using common sense. There is a famous anecdote about this:

The Reason

THERE WAS ONCE a man who had been put in charge of a study group. He decided to introduce supposedly 'spiritual exercises' and took some from a book. The people all became excited, and they all thought that something important was 'moving in them'. Then this group leader read somewhere else that it was only after people were not excited by exercises that they could develop higher understanding. So he carried on the exercises to look for such people. Most of them just became more and more hysterical. But one never seemed to be affected at all.

'Well,' said our hero to himself, 'at least we have one real student here.'

When the music and dancing and jumping up and down and swaying were finished for the evening, he went up to the man and asked him to follow him into his private room, so that they could have a talk.

The man cupped his hand to his ear, 'What did you say?' he asked...

What is Missing

Q: I have studied six religions, psychological and mystical systems as deeply as I could, and several others to a lesser extent. Each time I have come to the conclusion that something is missing from them...

A: Perhaps you would be interested if we put up against this reaction the fact that there is also a contrary side. By this I mean, of course, that every single religion, psychology and mystical system can provide numerous examples of people who feel the exact opposite. Such system, they hold, not only has nothing missing: it contains, for them, everything – and all the others are probably, by the same token, 'lacking' something.

People who believe that they will find something in a thing will tend to find it: and this includes such things as contentment with a system. People, on the other hand, who have something missing (or not yet found) in themselves and exteriorise this sense are looking for imperfection even in something they are studying. They will bring this sense of lack to the subject in question, and will attribute this sense of something missing to the materials, the people, the system. In more recent years – say the past forty or fifty – there has been a growing understanding of this syndrome, while it is not uncommon to read in former times of people who were obviously misfits drifting from one thing to another and calling everyone and everything else a misfit, or incomplete. Yet Rumi, for instance, clearly says 700 years ago: 'The lack is in you, fortunate one, and not in It or Them…'

The very act of finding things or other people unsatisfactory is in itself a partial therapy for this condition. It is a temporarily effective (though logically and in reality fallacious) solution to the perplexity situation: 'I can't find whatever I am looking for because it is not there at all. It must be somewhere else.' This is, quite simply, one of the options in any study or search. Another one is, of course, 'I am too stupid to understand it,' a third, 'I will find out in due course,' and a fourth, 'I must try harder.'

The unconscious projection of one's own problems onto others helps to reduce tension. But what about the real situation? If the projection, the self-therapy, also becomes a fixed belief that it is true, it may prevent people from actually sticking to something long enough to benefit from it; or it may make them seek more therapy, more and more fads and systems, to get the little bit of satisfaction that comes through the self-fulfilling prophecy that 'there is nothing there, it is incomplete...' This is an example of the remedy being a palliative for the disease. The only remedy to dependence on a temporary anodyne is to see that this is what you are doing, where you really are. Because people are not always in a condition to come to this realisation by an act of will, traditional psychologies provide methods and materials in which there is a possibility of seeing oneself as one really is. The opportunity occurs again and again, through the nature of such a curriculum, and it takes many forms.

The forms include literature and the company of other people under circumstances which exclude the urgency to understand instantly or to find complete systems. This may produce the intellectual paradox that you will find the completeness if you are not looking for it: but this is only because the original ailment was to look for something that one did not really want to find. So you can't blame the teaching, you have to look at the student's state.

The ordinary reaction to such information as 'look at the student, not at the teaching' is for the student to feel guilty or abashed or otherwise to adopt a non-constructive approach. He or she does this only because early training has implanted a signal that a reproach from a source of authority must be responded to by repentance or self-reproach. But self-observation is not the same as self-reproach. There is no harm in being abashed or subject to a sense of personal duty to do something. But when this takes the form of an automatic reaction, without the individual having any option to act or think otherwise, all that is happening is automatism.

Almost by definition, I would have said, a student lacks something. That is why he IS a student. He probably lacks many things. One of the things which many students lack – and it is no shame so to be – is the capacity to evaluate whether a teaching is complete or not; to evaluate, that is, the teaching itself. In order to miss something, to perceive incompleteness, you must know the thing which you are missing, know the complete thing.

It is generally, by the way, the thing that people 'want' not what they may at any given stage 'need' which they 'miss' or 'find wanting'.

To be really constructive, it is not too much to say that the sense that something is missing is not an occasion to abandon something or to reproach oneself for being inadequate. It is the occasion to gain all-important information that this state of mind is one which needs information about itself, and why it thinks like this. Following such information, when it has been thought about, the student can start to make the kind of approaches, and ask the kind of questions, which really enable him or her to learn, instead of revolving within inaccurate concepts.

Understanding

Q: *As you know, there are many people, throughout the world, inducing experiences in others, and giving them thereby what are felt to be priceless endowments. Why do the true Sufis not do this – surely there is an advantage in feeling exalted, or contact with the Higher Beings?*

A: These experiences are subjective and deceptive. If you care to come and sit with me for a few days, you will actually meet long processions of people who call themselves spiritual, and who constantly bemoan their loss of these feelings, formerly engendered and so welcomed by them when 'presented' or 'given' by what they regard as higher sources, whether material teachers or immaterial forces. This is the reality, not the occasional person who is still (and temporarily) in a state of exaltation of emotion.

This problem is, as Imam Ghazzali explains in the Third Book of his *Revival of Religious Sciences*, that these experiences are assuaging greed, not replacing it. He relates the Parable of

THE CUP OF RARE PEARLS

SOMEONE ONE DAY presented to a King a most valuable cup, made by joining together numerous rare pearls, and the King was delighted with it. Showing it to a courtier who was also a man of wisdom, the monarch asked him his opinion of it.

'This is a calamity,' said the other man.

'How can that be so?' asked the astonished King.

'If it happens to be broken,' said the courtier, 'you will bitterly regret it, since you will not be able to replace it. If it is stolen, you will miss it excruciatingly.'

And it did indeed happen that the cup was lost. Thus did the King realise the truth of what the wise man had said. And thus it is, says the Imam, with all things of this world.

Simply because one imagines that something which one has is spiritual does not make one's experience of it outside of this world. Indeed, the Sufi teachers constantly speak of the bitterness of deprivation, in order to emphasise this distinction: though people think that they are speaking about themselves.

Crazes

Q: *There is a craze to call oneself a Sufi, in the West. At the same time, there are many reputable people in Europe and America who are connected with the Sufis. How can we make sure that the craze does not spoil the name and work of the Sufis?*

A: From time to time, there is a craze for almost everything somewhere. The craze dies out, and people do not in any case usually assume that oddities are truly representative of the thing itself. For instance, there is a vegetarian craze, but this does not give vegetables a bad name: it only means that some people are more or less obsessed by vegetables. The craze for pornographic films does not endanger films, and so on.

The best safeguard is for normal people to treat the craze – and the crazies – in the way which they deserve. This is easy for us, since the Sufis and Sufism have a reputable ancestry and many normal adherents.

Your anxiety may perhaps be allayed by looking at a story which reports something which happened recently.

At a diplomatic reception in Bonn, a woman waitress spilt a tray of drinks over a distinguished Middle Eastern ambassador, who happens to be a Sufi.

She said: 'Do forgive me. You see, I am a Sufi. I am not a waitress!'

The diplomat looked at her and answered: 'You thought that you were a Sufi and not a waitress. Well, you may be assured that not only are you not a Sufi, but *you* really are a waitress!'

Sinning Against God and Man

SOMEONE ASKS ME how on earth anyone can have any respect for the Sufis, when it is reported that they hold that 'You can sin against God, but not against man'.

This kind of question provides an ideal opportunity to show how wildly the obsessives who have taken Sufis as their targets will (often unknowingly) distort the facts, and also to recall a very delightful lesson given by one of the ancients.

This lesson, valid to this day, is reported of Sheikh Ahmad of Manyar,* in Bihar, India, who was born in the thirteenth century, the seventh century of the Islamic Era. It is upon the evidence of this story that the allegation against the Sufis is based.

A man once visited the Sheikh and not knowing that he was fasting, offered him some food. To refuse food is a discourtesy, and the Sheikh immediately ate some.

Literalists who were present at once asked the Sufi how he could so lightly break an undertaking made to God.

The Sheikh answered:

*   Sheikh Ahmad Sharafuddin Ibn Yahya Manyari, recorded in the *Manaqib al-Asfiyya*.

'God will forgive the breaking of a fast; but how can one compensate a man for breaking his heart?'

In the eyes of the Sufi, a sin against a man, which may include distressing him, is also a 'sin against God'. This kind of thinking, however, is generally appreciated only feebly – if at all – by formalists who are, in reality, frequently less 'people of religion' than 'people of idolatry'. Their idolatry is to the limited number of observances and principles which they recognise, without perceiving the principle which underlies all.

A Request

If you enjoyed this book, please review it on Amazon and Goodreads.

Reviews are an author's best friend.

To stay in touch with news on forthcoming editions of Idries Shah works, please sign up for the mailing list:

http://bit.ly/ISFlist

And to follow him on social media, please go to any of the following links:

https://twitter.com/idriesshah

https://www.facebook.com/IdriesShah

http://www.youtube.com/idriesshah999

http://www.pinterest.com/idriesshah/

http://bit.ly/ISgoodreads

http://idriesshah.tumblr.com

https://www.instagram.com/idriesshah/

http://idriesshahfoundation.org

www.ingramcontent.com/pod-product-compliance
Lightning Source LLC
Chambersburg PA
CBHW020603030426
42337CB00013B/1185